★ This book belongs to ★

_____

KYAN KNIGHT

Note to Parents — If English is not your first language, please translate the text in this book into your first language and write the translations on the lines provided. Read the book with your child and share it with his or her classroom teacher. Students who see their languages and cultures valued by teachers and parents are more likely to feel confident at school.

 Ru'bĭcon © 2009 Rubicon Publishing Inc.
www.rubiconpublishing.com

Art Director: Rebecca Buchanan
Design: Jennifer Drew

10 11 12 13 14   6 5 4 3 2

ISBN: 978-1-55448-773-8

Paper used in the production of this book is a natural, recyclable product made from wood grown in sustainable forests. The manufacturing process conforms to the environmental regulations of the country of origin.

Coming to Kindergarten

By Michelle Gioskos • Suzanne Muir • Karamjit Sangha-Bosland
Art by Mernie Gallagher-Cole

(Draw a picture or paste a photo of yourself here.)

My name is _____

_____

4

(Draw a picture or paste a photo of your teacher here.)

My teacher's name is _____

_____

These are my friends!

_____

(Draw a picture of your friends here and write their names.)

My Day in
Kindergarten

I get ready for school.

Help us find our way to Kindergarten.

Welcome to Kindergarten!

I go to school.

I bring my backpack.

I line up.

I hang up my jacket and put away my backpack.

I sit on the carpet.

I raise my hand to talk.

We play in the classroom.

We work in the classroom.

I ask, "May I go to the washroom?"

I wash my hands.

I eat my snack.

I clean up after my snack.

We put on our outdoor clothes and shoes.

We play outside.

We make music.

We listen to a story.

We tidy up.

We say goodbye.

Picture Communication Symbols

line up

sit still

circle time

quiet

listen

book

washroom

wash hands

nutrition break

happy	sad	sick
water table	painting	art
blocks	sand table	house centre
tidy up	home time	school bus